EXTREME MACHINES

EXTREME OFF-ROAD VEHICLES

IAN F. MAHANEY

PowerKiDS press

New York

Published in 2016 by
The Rosen Publishing Group, Inc.
29 East 21st Street, New York, NY 10010

Developed and produced for Rosen by BlueAppleWorks Inc.

Art Director: T. J. Choleva
Managing Editor for BlueAppleWorks: Melissa McClellan
Designer: Stacie Ueno
Photo Research: Stacie Ueno/Jane Reid
Editor: Janice Dyer

Photo Credits:
Cover U.S. Marine Corps photo/Sgt. Jason W. Fudge/Public Domain; title page Maindru Photo/Creative Commons; p. 4 Laurentiu Iordache/Dreamstime; p. 4–5 Norwegian Army/Creative Commons; p. 5 top Antonella865/Dreamstime; p. 6 Johann Ragnarsson/Dreamstime; p. 6–7 Martin Kozak/Buggyra 2015/Keystone Press; p. 7 top Andres Rodriguez/Dreamstime; p. 7 bottom Edurivero/Dreamstime; p. 8–9 Vadim Rymakov/Keystone Press; p. 8 TZorn/Creative Commons; p. 9 Dionisius Purba/Creative Commons; p. 10–11 Rvannatta/Creative Commons; p. 11 Fanny Schertzer/Creative Commons; p. 12 Enruta/Dreamstime; p. 12–13, 13 NASA/Public Domain; p. 14 top left Bureau of Land Management/Creative Commons; p. 14 bottom left Emgallagher/Dreamstime; p. 14 right Sandago/Dreamstime; p. 14–15 Christian Lagereek/Dreamstime; p. 15 top Myron Reynard/Creative Commons; p. 16 Clemens Vasters/Creative Commons; p. 16–17 Tim Green/Creative Commons; p. 17 top Comyu/Creative Commons; p. 18 left Lazyllama/Dreamstime; p. 18 right Jacqueline Abromeit/Shutterstock; p. 18–19 Fergy/Dreamstime; p. 19 top Tr3gi/Dreamstime; p. 19 bottom U.S. Navy photo/Photographer's Mate 1st Class Arlo Abrahamson/Public Domain; p. 20 left VanderWolf Images/Dreamstime; p. 20–21 U.S. Air Force photo/Tech. Sgt. H. H. Deffner/Public Domain; p. 21 top Theresa Martinez/Dreamstime; p. 22 left Andrew Skudder/Creative Commons; p. 23 top Michael Adams/Dreamstime; p. 22–23 U.S. Marine Corps photo/Joseph A. Lambach/Public Domain; p. 24 left 7th Army Joint Multinational Training Command/Creative Commons; p. 24 right AlfvanBeem/Creative Commons; p. 24–25 Jose Ferrufino, U.S. Army/Public Domain; p. 26 U.S. Air Force photo/Senior Airman Eric Harris/Public Domain; p. 27 top U.S. Air Force photo/Staff Sgt. Jason T. Bailey/Public Domain; p. 27 Robert Sholl/Dreamstime; p.28 Johnnydao/Dreamstime; p. 28–29 U.S. Navy photo/PH1 Scott Allen/Public Domain; p. 29 top Xxlphoto/Dreamstime; p. 29 bottom Vitaly V. Kuzmin/Creative Commons.

Cataloging-in-Publication-Data
Mahaney, Ian F.
Extreme off-road vehicles / by Ian F. Mahaney.
p. cm. — (Extreme machines)
Includes index.
ISBN 978-1-4994-1185-0 (pbk.)
ISBN 978-1-4994-1213-0 (6 pack)
ISBN 978-1-4994-1212-3 (library binding)
1. Off-road vehicles — Juvenile literature. I. Mahaney, Ian F. II. Title.
TL235.6 M3484 2016
629.22'042—d23

Manufactured in the United States of America
CPSIA Compliance Information: Batch #WS15PK: For Further Information contact: Rosen Publishing, New York, New York at 1-800-237-9932

Contents

What Are Off-Road Vehicles?

Cars, trucks, and motorcycles that can travel on many surfaces are called off-road vehicles. Like regular vehicles, many off-road vehicles can drive on smooth paved surfaces like streets and highways. Off-road vehicles, though, can go where passenger cars can't go. Off-road vehicles are made to drive on natural surfaces like dirt, mud, sand, and snow. These cars, trucks, motorcycles, and other vehicles have mighty engines that power the vehicles through mud or over rocks.

Some off-road vehicles have huge tires that grip uneven surfaces. Other off-road vehicles have deep treads in their tires that allow the vehicles to grab hold of tough **terrain**. The treads also clear water, sand, and mud from the tires. Many off-road vehicles have caterpillar tracks. Caterpillar tracks are long metal and rubber treads that grip natural surfaces and allow the vehicles to stay on top of mud, dirt, and snow. This keeps these vehicles moving.

Bucket-wheel excavators are used for mining. They move massive amounts of earth and rocks.

Powerful Machines

Extreme off-road vehicles are powerful vehicles that can handle the toughest conditions and do lots of hard work. They include tanks and bulldozers, **snowcats**, and dune buggies. Some off-road vehicles take people on **safaris**. Other extreme off-road vehicles can even drive on land, then into the water.

Off-road vehicles will take you through desert and jungle, over rocks, and through grassland.

Powerful tracked vehicles are also used by armies to transport soldiers through tough terrain.

The Best of the Best

People often compete in races. They run races on foot. They race on ice skates and bikes. People race cars and other motorized vehicles. People also race off-road vehicles.

Formula Off Road is extreme off-road racing that is popular in **Nordic countries** like Iceland and Norway. In Formula Off Road, drivers race trucks up steep hills. Many of these trucks have huge paddle tires that are good for digging in dirt and getting a grip on loose surfaces. These vehicles must be powerful and sturdy. They climb such steep hills that the trucks sometimes flip over and slide down the hills.

Formula Off Road races usually take place in closed areas like rock mines.

The Dakar Rally crosses sand dunes, mud, rocks, and grass. The vehicles are specially designed to drive on off-road terrain.

Dakar Rally

Another extreme off-road race is the Dakar Rally. The Dakar Rally is a race that lasts about two weeks and has many stages. A stage at Dakar is a one-day race that can be as long as 600 miles (970 km). Originally, the Dakar Rally was a race from Paris, France, to Dakar, Senegal. Since 2009, the Dakar Rally has been held in South America. Drivers compete to win in four categories. The categories are cars, trucks, motorcycles, and quads. Quads are also called all-terrain vehicles. They are small off-road vehicles that hold a driver and up to three passengers.

Hardworking Machines

Haul Trucks

Even though some haul trucks are the size of a small apartment building, they can still move well on rough terrain.

Mining is a business where companies and workers dig in the earth to find valuable **resources** like coal and gold. Companies and workers use machines to dig for these materials. The machines also dig up a lot of dirt and rock. Haul trucks are huge off-road vehicles that remove this waste. Some haul trucks are so big that the drivers use a ladder to climb into the **cab**.

True Giants

The Caterpillar 797F is one of the biggest and most powerful haul trucks on Earth. It is more than 25 feet (7.6 m) tall, almost 50 feet (15 m) long, and its ground clearance is more than 2.5 feet (0.8 m). Ground clearance is important for off-road vehicles. The ground clearance is the distance between the ground and the underside of the vehicle. When an off-road vehicle has a large clearance it can keep away from damaging rocks on the ground.

The Belaz 75710 is an even larger haul truck. It has eight tires, each more than 13 feet (4 m) tall. That's about as tall as the world's tallest elephants. The Belaz 75710 also has a payload of 495 tons (450 metric tons). A truck's payload is the amount of weight it can carry. The Belaz 75710 could carry 40 big elephants.

Logging Trucks

Tractor trailers are powerful trucks used to haul freight on highways. These trucks have two parts. The tractor is an engine and cab where the driver sits. The trailer is a long box that holds cargo.

Logging trucks are special tractor trailers with pole trailers. The pole trailers are filled with logs. Instead of having walls like the boxes of normal trailers, pole trailers hold their cargo using metal stakes.

Some logging trucks are tough off-road trucks. Off-road logging trucks carry trees out of the woods. They haul their loads through dirt and mud, and over rocks.

Off-road logging trucks need to be able to climb hills and travel through mud, snow, gravel, and soil.

Did You Know?

In many parts of the world a logging truck is called a timber lorry.

Logging trucks use special cranes to load the logs. The logs are unloaded by letting them roll off the truck.

Self-Loading Trucks

Truck companies can **customize** trucks when customers order them. Some logging trucks are customized to be self loaders. Self loaders are trucks that have their own cranes. The Western Star 4900 is an example of an off-road pole trailer that has a self-loading crane. The 4900 can drive into the woods and load logs itself. Then the logging truck hauls the load through the mud and out of the woods.

Tracked Power Machines

Caterpillar tracks are also called continuous tracks. Off-road vehicles with tracks have many military and **civilian** uses. Tracked vehicles push snow around at ski resorts. Other tracked vehicles move dirt and mud for construction projects. Snowmobiles are small off-road vehicles powered by continuous tracks. Some companies make continuous tracked cars. Other companies and mechanics **modify** cars, trucks, and vans so the vehicles can travel in deep snow.

In warmer places, companies build continuous tracked vehicles to take tourists into swamps and marshes. These vehicles can cross rivers and climb over rocks and small hills. Continuous tracked vehicles also help in relief efforts after tidal waves, floods, and earthquakes. Tracked vehicles like bulldozers are useful for cleaning up debris.

A bulldozer is a continuous tracked vehicle that is used to push large quantities of sand, soil, rock, or other material.

The Biggest of All

One of the biggest tracked vehicles ever made moved the United States space shuttles on a gravel track. The crawler-transporter carried shuttles from their **hangar** to the launch pad at the Kennedy Space Center. The Kennedy Space Center is in Cape Canaveral, Florida. The crawler-transporter has eight tracks, weighs 5.5 million pounds (2.5 million kg), and can carry a space shuttle with rocket boosters weighing 4.5 million pounds (2 million kg).

It took the crawler-transporter about 6 hours to move the Space Shuttle *Atlantis* to its launch pad, a distance of 3.4 miles (5.5 km). The crawler-transporter travels on eight tracks, and each track has 57 individual "shoes" that make up the tread.

Mighty Tractors

Tractors are farm machines that help farmers work. Most tractors have two small wheels in the front of the vehicle and two big wheels in the back. The big wheels have deep grooved tires that help the tractor move through mud, sand, and dirt while towing another heavy machine.

Tractors move slowly when they tow heavy equipment like plows or **combines**. Tractors can drive through mud and dirt, and haul their loads through these off-road conditions. They can also turn quickly because they have two brake pedals. Each brake controls one back wheel. The driver can stop one wheel while letting the other wheel roll and turn.

Large tractors are mostly used for farming. They are also used in garbage dump sites and other workplaces.

Montana Giant

Tractors can be small or very large. The biggest tractor ever made is called Big Bud 16V 747. Big Bud was made in Montana in 1977 and produced 760 horsepower. Horsepower is a unit of measure that tells you the amount of work an engine can do. Originally, 1 horsepower meant an engine could do the work of one horse. Since 1977, Big Bud has been modified so that it can produce even more horsepower. Big Bud is much bigger than a normal tractor. It is 14 feet (4.3 m) tall and has 8 giant wheels.

The first engine-powered tractor was built in 1892. Today, companies are working on building a driverless tractor.

Across Water and Sand

Amphibious Vehicles

An amphibian is an animal that lives part of its life on land and part of its life in water. Amphibious vehicles are off-road vehicles that can travel on land and also in water. They can drive on a highway, cross a sandy beach, and splash into a lake or ocean.

The United States Navy and Marines began testing amphibious vehicles in the 1930s. By 1941, when the United States entered **World War II**, the Navy and Marines were using the DUKW. This amphibious vehicle could sail like a ship on the ocean, climb over coral reefs, and drive onto the beach. Once on the beach, the DUKW could drive on the rest of an island. The Marines continue to use amphibious vehicles today.

The DUKW was the first vehicle that allowed the driver to change the tire pressure from inside the vehicle. Tires are fully inflated for driving on hard roads, and less inflated for softer surfaces.

Most Amphicars were sold in the United States. Owners get together every July to celebrate their vehicles at events called "swim-ins."

AB-G192

Extreme Joyrides

There are amphibious vehicles for civilians, too. One of the first amphibious cars was called the Amphicar. They were made in the 1960s and could drive 70 miles (113 km) per hour on the highway. Once the Amphicar entered the water, two propellers powered the car and it could travel at 9 miles (14.5 km) per hour. Amphicars have crossed the English Channel and traveled off the California coast from San Diego to Catalina Island.

Amphibious cars are much faster today. The Watercar Python is an amphibious car with a Corvette engine and can speed more than 57 miles (92 km) per hour in the water.

Off-Road Sandrails

Many off-road vehicles can drive in sand. All-terrain vehicles and trucks with big treaded tires drive on the beach. These vehicles can drive faster when the sand is harder and packed down with water. Dune buggies are off-road vehicles that are made for driving on sand. Dune buggies have no windows. Sometimes they have a roof, but other dune buggies have roll bars. A roll bar is a support above the driver and passengers that protects people if their dune buggy rolls over.

Some dune buggies are for work. Others are for fun. Sandrails are lightweight dune buggies that are made for fun. They are off-road vehicles with large rear tires. These tires power the sandrail so it can drive fast in sand dunes and other areas of open sand.

Dune buggies are also called beach buggies. They are usually modified from an existing vehicle, often a Volkswagen Beetle.

Sandrails for Tourists

Larger sandrails can take more passengers for rides in the dunes. Some sandrails can fit nine passengers.

The U.S. military uses sandrails when patrolling the desert.

Made to Fit

People often buy kits or plans to make their open sand vehicles. There are even books that teach people how to build their own sandrails.

Sandrails can fit a driver and one or more passengers. A sandrail's speed is limited by dune speed limits. The speed limit is often 55 miles (89 km) per hour.

Military Super Machines

U.S. Military Classic– The Jeep

The U.S. Army used the first Jeeps in World War II. The army needed these lightweight off-road vehicles to transport troops near battlefields and to watch enemy movements. The first Jeeps could hold a driver and three passengers. Jeeps have grooved tires, powerful engines, and four-wheel drive. Four-wheel-drive cars and trucks have engines that power all four wheels of the vehicle. Four-wheel-drive vehicles are also called 4x4s. In most cars and trucks, the engine only powers one or two of the wheels.

The army also used Jeeps to move small amounts of cargo and to scout routes that heavier trucks and tanks would drive. Two American automobile companies, Willys and Ford, made more than 600,000 Jeeps for the United States during the war. The Jeeps weighed 2,450 pounds (1,110 kg) each, and were fast. They could shuttle troops away from the enemy at up to 65 miles (105 km) per hour. Some Jeeps even had guns mounted on their hoods.

Jeeps were used for many purposes during World War II. Some were used as firefighting pumpers or field ambulances. Others were used to lay cable or to run on railway tracks.

The first Jeeps were produced in 1941 for the military.

The military continued to use Jeeps after World War II. Here, soldiers in Operation Desert Shield are giving a missile demonstration in Jeep YJ light vehicles.

Civilian Drivers

U.S. armed forces have used Jeeps since World War II, but Jeeps are mainly used as civilian cars today. Jeeps can drive well on highways, but they can also handle many off-road conditions.

All-Powerful Tanks

Tanks are large fighting machines that countries around the world use in battle. They are heavily armored vehicles that move on continuous tracks and have large guns or cannons on their roofs.

The British made the first tank in 1915. It was called Little Willie. It weighed 14 tons (13 metric tons) and moved slowly. In 1916, the first tank entered the battlefield for the British during **World War I**. The tank was named Big Willie and it was designed to cross large trenches.

Tanks were important weapons in World War II. Many nations such as the United States, the Soviet Union, and Germany used tanks because they had heavy armor and could drive off-road.

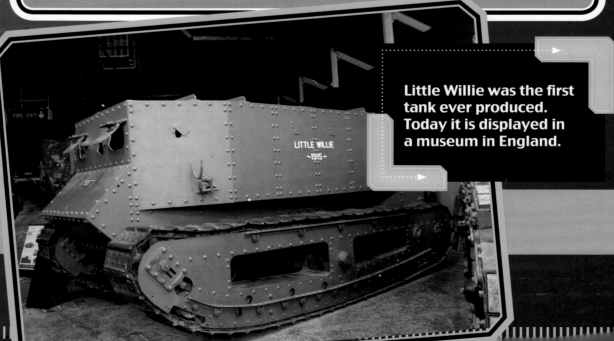

LITTLE WILLIE ~1915~

Little Willie was the first tank ever produced. Today it is displayed in a museum in England.

This M247 Sergeant York DIVAD was developed in the 1970s. It was named after Sergeant Alvin York, a famous World War I hero.

The Abrams M1A1 guns have a range of 8,200 feet (2,500 m). They were used during the Gulf War in the 1990s.

Mighty Abrams

Today's tanks are fast and powerful weapons. The United States' M1 Abrams tanks are extreme modern tanks. They are made of steel and other materials to protect them from enemy fire. Abrams tanks are 32 feet (9.75 m) long and weigh 63 tons (57 metric tons) when filled with four crew members, fuel, and ammunition. Abrams tanks can speed along at 42 miles (68 km) per hour and their ground clearance is 19 inches (48 cm). Abrams tanks can cross streams, drive through a desert, and handle other off-road terrain.

Armored Bulldozers

Bulldozers are powerful tractors with wide metal blades that are used for pushing dirt and rocks. Bulldozers have tracks for working in off-road environments like mines and on construction sites.

Military forces around the world use bulldozers, too. In battle zones, these bulldozers are modified and fitted with armor. Allies like Great Britain and the United States used armored bulldozers in World War II. During the Battle of Normandy in 1944, the Allies used Caterpillar D7 armored bulldozers to move obstacles on the beaches and push sand into antitank ditches, so their tanks could cross the beaches and drive into mainland Europe. Armored bulldozers can also move sand to build barriers and rescue damaged fighting vehicles.

Newer models of the Caterpillar D7 are still used in the military today.

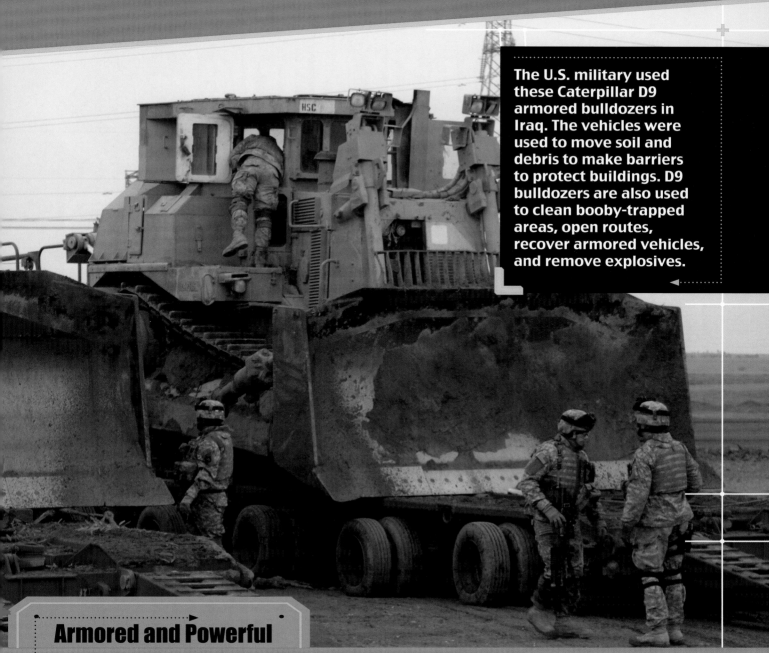

The U.S. military used these Caterpillar D9 armored bulldozers in Iraq. The vehicles were used to move soil and debris to make barriers to protect buildings. D9 bulldozers are also used to clean booby-trapped areas, open routes, recover armored vehicles, and remove explosives.

Armored and Powerful

The allies also used tankdozers in World War II. Tankdozers are tanks with bulldozer blades attached to the front. The British used their Centaur tanks with bulldozer blades to clear debris. The United States also used M4 Sherman tanks with bulldozer blades.

Armed forces around the world still use armored bulldozers today. Israel uses armored Caterpillar D9 bulldozers to clear mines and other obstacles while under fire. The United States used the same D9 armored bulldozers during the Iraq War known as Operation Iraqi Freedom.

Off-Road Marvel– the Humvee

The U.S. Armed Forces use Humvees to transport cargo or small numbers of troops. The Armed Forces **collaborated** with auto manufacturer AM General to make Humvees. These four-wheel-drive trucks first entered service for the U.S. military in 1985. Humvees can be armored and have bulletproof windows.

Humvees can carry machine guns or missile launchers. They can also be modified and turned into ambulances. Humvees can rush injured troops to the hospital at 70 miles (113 km) per hour. They are also awesome off-road vehicles. Humvees can drive off-road in desert conditions, through the jungle, or in snow. Humvees have 16 inches (41 cm) of ground clearance and can cross water up to 2.5 feet (0.8 m) deep. Humvees can also climb steep hills and carry a payload of 5,100 pounds (2,300 kg).

Humvees can easily and quickly travel across the desert and across rough terrain. Over 10,000 of these vehicles were used during the Iraq War.

Fast-Moving HMMWV

Since Humvees are quick, they are used to explore areas. They can also be fitted with communications equipment so they can speak with troops in other vehicles.

Humvee is a nickname for these extreme off-road vehicles. The Humvee's official name is High Mobility Multipurpose Wheeled Vehicle. Its initials are HMMWV. The letters in Humvee and HMMWV are **similar**.

This Humvee in Afghanistan has a special radio antenna on the back. This device scans the area looking for signals from improvised explosive devices.

Off-Road, Off-Land Hovercrafts

Hovercrafts are incredible off-road vehicles that float above flat surfaces like swamps, dirt, and snow. Hovercrafts float above flat surfaces by creating cushions of air between the vehicle and the surface below. Because of the cushion, hovercrafts are also called ACVs or air-cushioned vehicles. Hovercrafts create the air cushion by changing the air pressure beneath the vehicle. The air pressure beneath the vehicle is higher than the air pressure above the vehicle. This lifts hovercrafts in the air. It is similar to how airplanes create lift and fly in the air.

Hovercrafts are used by civilians for recreation. They are also used by governments around the world for military purposes, and in search and rescue operations. The U.S. Navy and Marines use hovercrafts to deliver troops and vehicles to shore.

This hovercraft is transporting cargo and personnel from ship to shore and across beaches.

Hovercrafts are often used to help with disaster relief during floods. They can also be used to transport civilians.

Fast Machines

The fastest hovercraft reached 85 miles (137 km) per hour over water in 1995. The fastest speed over land was 56 miles (90 km) per hour in 1998.

The Zubr-class LCAC is the largest type of hovercraft. Several countries use these vehicles, including Russia, Ukraine, Greece, and China.

Russian Giants

The biggest hovercrafts are Ukrainian military hovercrafts known as Zubr hovercrafts. The Zubr hovercrafts are 187 feet (57 m) long and weigh 550 tons (500 metric tons). They can carry three main battle tanks, or ten armored vehicles with 140 troops.

GLOSSARY

cab The space where truck drivers sit.

civilian People who are not in the military.

collaborated Worked together.

combines Farm machines that harvest grain.

customize To make changes to something.

hangar A shed used for storing aircraft.

modify To change.

Nordic countries Denmark, Iceland, Norway, Sweden, and Finland in northern Europe.

resources Things that occur in nature and that can be used or sold, such as gold, coal, or wool.

safaris Journeys through Africa to see the land and animals.

similar Almost the same as.

snowcats Big tracked vehicles that drive on top of snow.

terrain A piece of land.

World War I The war fought between the Allies and the Central powers from 1914 to 1918.

World War II The war fought by the United States, Great Britain, France, and the Soviet Union against Germany, Japan, and Italy from 1939 to 1945.

Further Reading

Brook, Henry. *Tanks.*
London, UK: Usborne Books, 2011.

David, Jack. *Humvees.*
Minneapolis, MN: Bellwether Media, 2009.

Hamilton, John. *Humvees.*
Edina, MN: ABDO Group, 2011.

Peppas, Lynn. *ATVs and Off-Roaders.*
New York, NY: Crabtree Publishing, 2012.

Shank, Carol. *U.S. Military Assault Vehicles.*
North Mankato, MN: Capstone Press, 2012.

Worms, Penny. *Off-road Vehicles.*
London, UK: Franklin Watts Ltd, 2013.

Websites

Due to the changing nature of Internet links, PowerKids Press has developed an online list of websites related to the subject of this book. This site is updated regularly. Please use this link to access the list: **www.powerkidslinks.com/em/offroad**

INDEX